AF231293

FRESH WATERS

Written by Izzi Howell

Illustrated by Steve Evans

WORLD BOOK

a Scott Fetzer company
Chicago

World Book, Inc.
180 North LaSalle Street
Suite 900
Chicago, Illinois 60601
USA

For information about other World Book publications,
visit our website at **www.worldbook.com**
or call **1-800-WORLDBK (967-5325)**.
For information about sales to schools and libraries,
call 1-800-975-3250 (United States),
or 1-800-837-5365 (Canada).

© 2023 World Book, Inc. All rights reserved. This
volume may not be reproduced in whole or in part
in any form without prior written permission from
the publisher.

WORLD BOOK and the GLOBE DEVICE are registered
trademarks or trademarks of World Book, Inc.

Library of Congress Cataloging-in-Publication Data
for this volume has been applied for.

Building Blocks of Geography
ISBN: 978-0-7166-4275-6 (set, hc.)

Fresh Waters
ISBN: 978-0-7166-4280-0 (hc.)

Also available as:
ISBN: 978-0-7166-4290-9 (e-book)

1st printing June 2022

WORLD BOOK STAFF
Executive Committee
President: Geoff Broderick
Vice President, Editorial: Tom Evans
Vice President, Finance: Donald D. Keller
Vice President, Marketing: Jean Lin
Vice President, International: Eddy Kisman
Vice President, Technology: Jason Dole
Director, Human Resources: Bev Ecker

Editorial
Manager, New Content: Jeff De La Rosa
Associate Manager, New Product:
    Nicholas Kilzer
Sr. Editor: Shawn Brennan
Proofreader: Nathalie Strassheim

Graphics and Design
Sr. Visual Communications Designer:
    Melanie Bender
Sr. Web Designer/Digital Media Developer:
    Matt Carrington
Coordinator, Design Development:
    Brenda Tropinski

Acknowledgments:
Writer: Izzi Howell
Illustrator: Steve Evans
Series advisor: Marjorie Frank

Developed with World Book by
White-Thomson Publishing LTD

www.wtpub.co.uk

TABLE OF CONTENTS

There is a glossary on page 40.
Terms defined in the glossary
are in type **that looks like this**
on their first appearance.

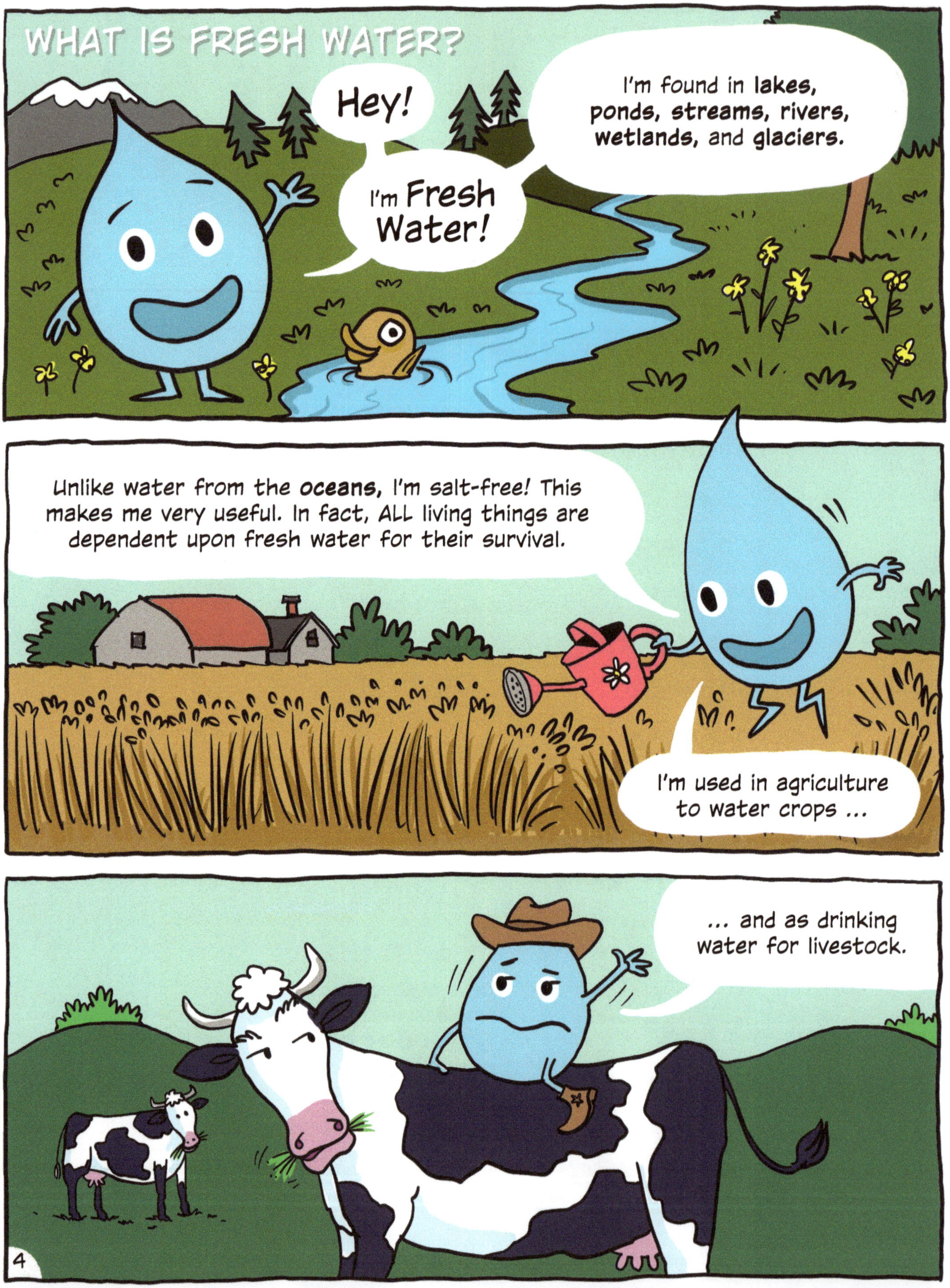

Hey!
I'm Fresh Water!
I'm found in lakes, ponds, streams, rivers, wetlands, and glaciers.
Unlike water from the oceans, I'm salt-free! This makes me very useful. In fact, ALL living things are dependent upon fresh water for their survival.
I'm used in agriculture to water crops ...
... and as drinking water for livestock.

I'm needed to generate electricity, and I'm used in the manufacturing of many products.

I'm in your cool, refreshing drink, your dishwasher ...

... and even your toilet!

From space, it looks like there's plenty of water on Earth. But fresh water only makes up a tiny amount of that water - about three percent.

So it's important to look after me and not use too much!

MAJOR FRESH WATERS

Fresh water is found in rivers and lakes all over the world.

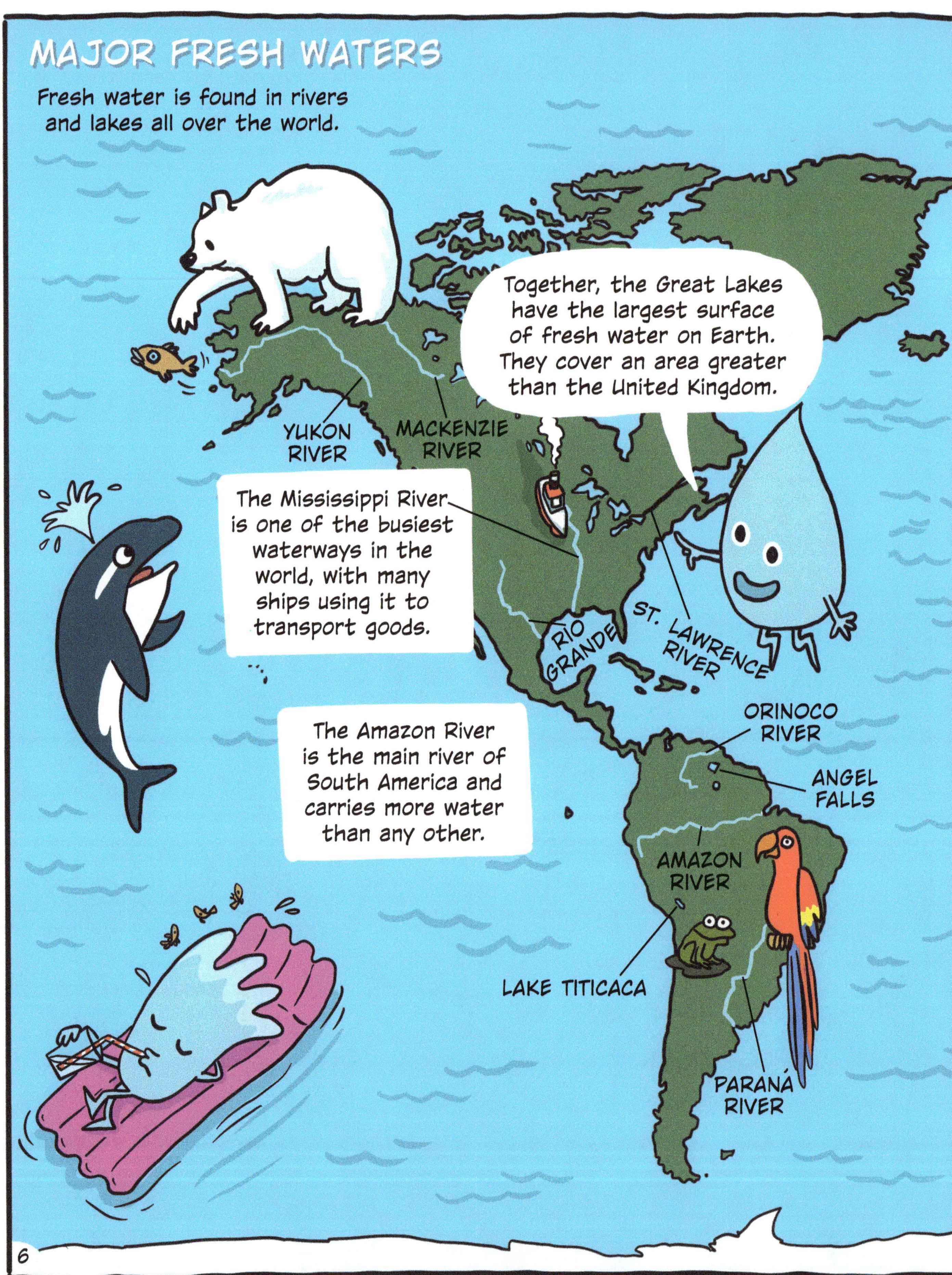

Lake Baikal is the deepest lake in the world. Its deepest point is around 5,300 feet (1,615 meters) down!
The Caspian Sea is technically the world's largest lake, but it's not actually fresh water! It's less salty than the ocean though.
The Nile River is the longest river in the world. It flows for 4,160 miles (6,695 kilometers) through northeast Africa.
OB RIVER
RHINE RIVER
DANUBE RIVER
INDUS RIVER
EUPHRATES RIVER
DEAD SEA
GANGES RIVER
NIGER RIVER
NILE RIVER
CONGO RIVER
MEKONG RIVER
ZAMBEZI RIVER
DARLING RIVER
MURRAY RIVER
LAMBERT GLACIER

RIVERS AND STREAMS
This little stream doesn't look like much, but it's actually the source of a mighty river.

But where does this water come from?

This stream is formed from melted ice and snow running down the side of the mountain.

The stream runs quickly downhill. It gets bigger as it connects to other small streams, or tributaries.
8

It is now a river!

Whoa, it's much bigger now!

As the river gains more water from tributaries and flows across flatter ground, it slows down. It becomes wider and deeper.

This is the river's mouth. No, not that kind of mouth!

A river's mouth is where it ends. Most rivers end by flowing into an ocean.

Let me show you some features that you can spot along the path of a river, such as **meanders** and **estuaries**.
Watch out for the bend!
Meanders like this form as the river water flows down its path.
Oh, hey! Just wave-ing hello to my friend Ocean!
We're always running into each other in estuaries! An estuary is a wide river mouth where fresh water mixes with **salt water** from the ocean.
Wow, look at this amazing river **delta**! Sediment has built up in the mouth of this river, splitting it into separate channels. Sediment is the soil, sand, and rocks that get carried along by the river.

Rivers don't just look cool. They're also really useful!

Rivers are important transport links.
People and goods travel on boats.

On some rivers there are hydroelectric dams that convert the energy from moving water into electricity.
Rivers might power the lights in your house!

No, corn doesn't come from rivers ...
... but rivers do help corn plants to grow!
When rivers flood, they leave behind sediment, which fertilizes the soil. Crops grow well in these areas.

WATERFALLS
There's nothing more relaxing than floating down a ri ...

Aahhh!

That waterfall came out of nowhere!
But now that I'm here at the bottom, let's take a closer look.
12

A waterfall is a place where a river flows over a ledge to a lower level below.
They can form when a river wears away the rock in different ways, leaving a high cliff followed by a drop.

And now I'm here, in the plunge pool at the bottom!

Watch out! The falling water can create whirlpools in the plunge pool.

Phew! Let's look at some different types of waterfalls while I catch my breath.

A cascade flows down rock steps.

A cataract is a very powerful and large waterfall.

A plunge waterfall doesn't touch the rock wall behind it.

Well, this is much calmer after that surprise waterfall adventure!

I'm on a lake – a large area of fresh water that is surrounded by land.

Lakes come in all different shapes and sizes.
Very small lakes are known as ponds.

Some larger lakes are called seas. These are often a little bit salty!

Some lakes get their water from rivers or streams.

Others are filled up by rain and **groundwater**.

Lakes form in holes in the ground, called basins.
Think of them as a bit like massive puddles!

Lake basins are formed in different ways.

Some basins were carved out by glaciers as they moved across the land thousands of years ago.

Other holes were left behind after volcanoes erupted.

Lake basins can also be created when parts of Earth's crust move and crack.

Humans can also make lakes! Sometimes they dig out a basin using machinery.

Lakes are also formed when people build a dam across a river.
Water is trapped behind the dam and floods the surrounding area, creating a new lake.

Lakes are pretty incredible. They contain 98 percent of the fresh water that is available to us!

Some towns and cities depend on lakes for their water supply.

Water from some lakes is used on farms and in factories.

Some lakes are popular places to swim and sail!

WATERSHEDS

The water in rivers and lakes comes from rain. Not only like this though!

Rain falls everywhere.

Gravity pulls the water downhill until it reaches a river or lake.

In this way, excess water is drained off the land. Otherwise, the land could become flooded.

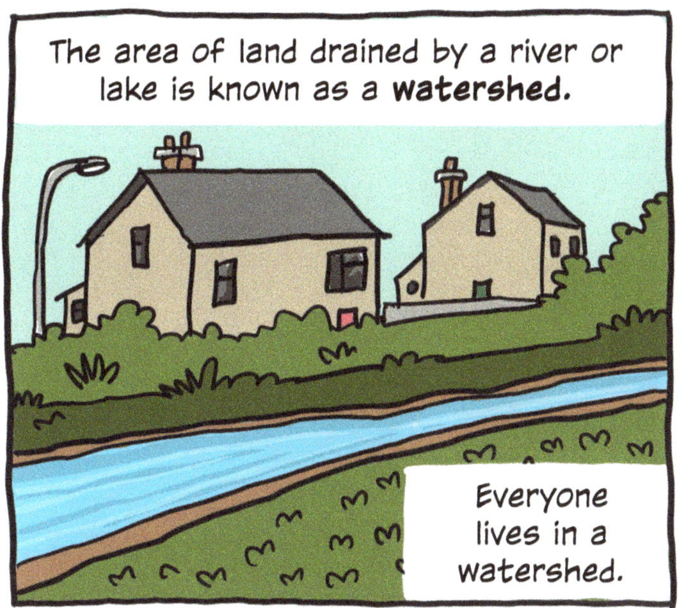

The area of land drained by a river or lake is known as a watershed.
Everyone lives in a watershed.

If you live in a town or city, rain may drain in a slightly different way!

Rain that falls on paved streets runs into storm drains.

Storm drains are connected to sewers, which release their water into streams and rivers.

Not all of the rain and melted snow that falls in a watershed is drained into rivers.
Some soaks into the ground and becomes groundwater.

A watershed can be very small. The watershed of this tiny brook is made up of just the slopes on either side of the valley.

But look — this brook is a tributary of a larger river.
A river's watershed includes the watersheds of all of its tributaries, so this tiny watershed isn't so little any more!

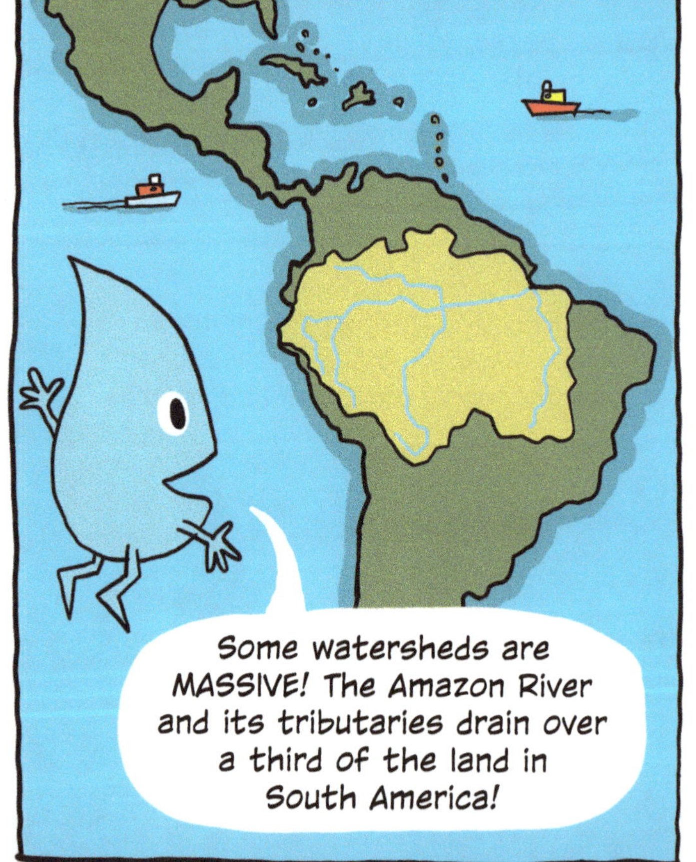

Some watersheds are MASSIVE! The Amazon River and its tributaries drain over a third of the land in South America!

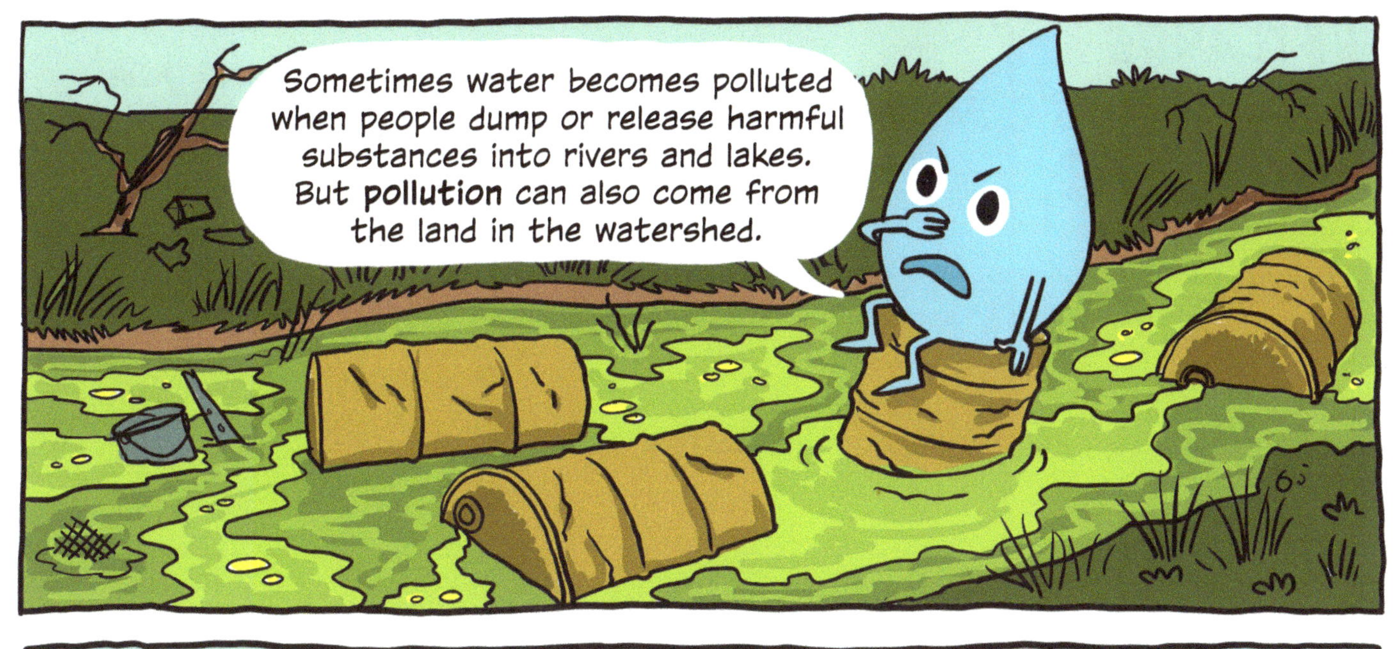
Sometimes water becomes polluted when people dump or release harmful substances into rivers and lakes. But **pollution** can also come from the land in the watershed.

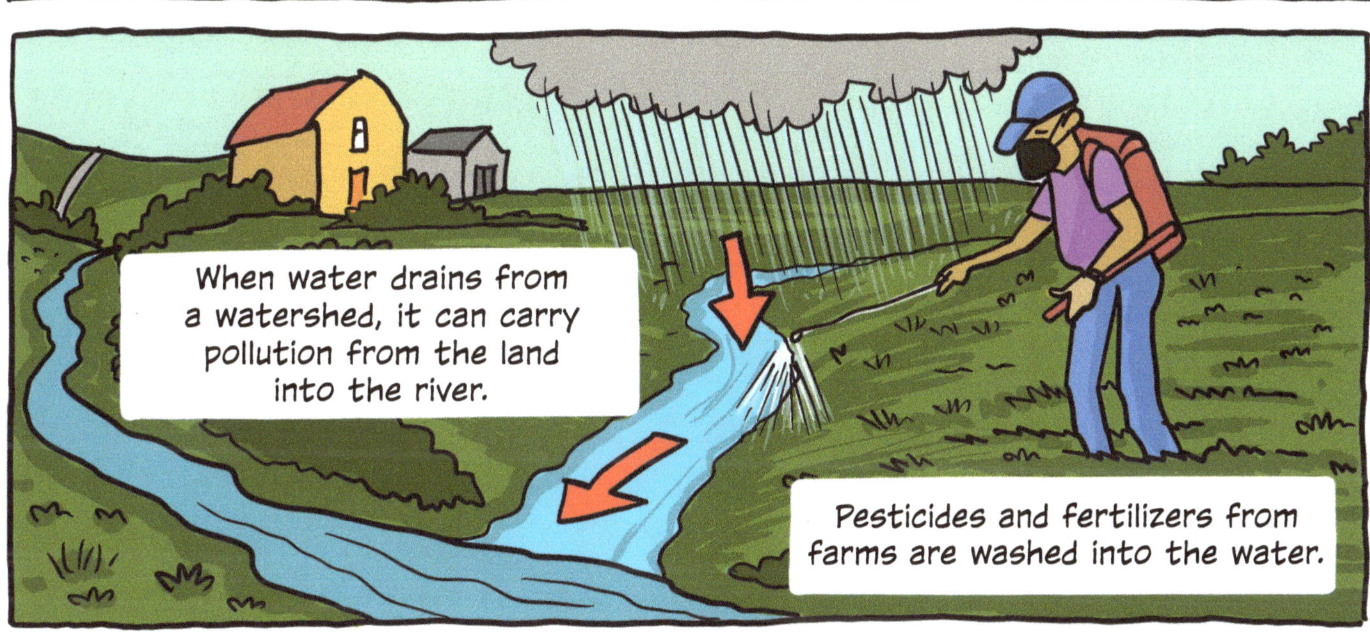
When water drains from a watershed, it can carry pollution from the land into the river.
Pesticides and fertilizers from farms are washed into the water.

Most of the pollution in water comes from waste or sewage produced by farms, factories or refineries, and cities. This pollution can hurt, and even kill, river animals and plants.

WETLANDS

Land or water?
It's hard to tell!

We must be in a wetland! These
are areas of land that are very ...
er ... wet! They are covered in
water for some of the year.

The water in wetlands
can come from
the ground ...

... a flooded
river ...

... or the
sea!

So the water in a wetland
can be fresh water, like
me, or a bit salty.
Remember
me?

This is a swamp. It has lots of trees and is usually covered in water.

Those wetlands didn't look like each other, right? That's because they are all different types of wetlands!

This is a marsh. The land is regularly covered by water and then exposed again. Lots of different grasses grow here.

This is a bog. Only a few plants grow here. Bogs are found in colder places than swamps and marshes.

Wetlands are very important **ecosystems**.
They are home to many species of plants and animals.

This makes them popular places to explore. People come to hike, kayak, and watch birds.

Many types of shellfish, such as crabs and oysters, are harvested from wetlands.

Wetlands have other superpowers too!

They absorb extra water during flooding.

They help to protect coastlines from storms.

They help to clean fresh water by filtering out waste.

But when people decide to build towns, resorts, or shopping malls on wetlands, they lose the benefits that these superpowers bring to protect the ecosystem.

GROUNDWATER
Around 30 percent of the fresh water on Earth is hiding underground! This underground water is called groundwater.
So how does the water get there?

Rain and melted snow soak through the soil.

The water fills all of the empty spaces in the soil and rock until it reaches solid rock that it can't pass through.

The layer of soil and rock that contains groundwater is called an **aquifer**. It's like a huge underground water warehouse!

Some groundwater slowly flows through the ground and into rivers and streams.

It can also burst out of the ground as a spring.

Groundwater is an important source of fresh water.
We use wells to get groundwater out of the aquifer.

Many rural areas without a main water supply depend on groundwater.

Groundwater saves the day in this dry desert with no rivers or lakes nearby!

Chemicals from farming and garbage dumps can pollute groundwater. If people use or drink polluted water, it can make them ill. Polluted groundwater can also harm wildlife and make the soil toxic (poisonous).

Careful! It's important not to pump out too much groundwater because wells can run dry. Then the benefits of groundwater are lost.

Hooray for rain! Now the groundwater will fill up again.

GLACIERS
Brrr... it's freezing up here!

But I've got something incredible to show you ... a glacier!
A glacier is a huge mass of ice that slowly moves across the land.

Glaciers form when layers of snow squash together under their own weight. This turns into very dense ice.

Glaciers are so heavy that their own weight pushes them along!

Some glaciers flow downhill through valleys. These are called mountain glaciers.

Mountain glaciers are found in high mountains around the world.
This glacier in the Himalayas is the source of the Ganges River, which flows through India and Bangladesh.

An ice sheet is a dome-shaped glacier spread across the landscape, covering everything in its path with ice.

About 91 percent of the glacier ice on Earth is in the Antarctic ice sheet!

Glaciers are very powerful! They can carry huge boulders ...

... cut valleys into mountains ...

...and wear away rock.

Most glaciers move around an inch (two and a half centimeters) a day. A few, like this galloping glacier, can move up to 160 feet (49 meters) a day!

Many glaciers are melting because of global warming.

The melted ice and snow flows into the sea and makes sea levels rise.
This leads to flooding in low areas.

Some pieces of melting glaciers break off and float out to sea as icebergs.

If climate change continues, glaciers may one day be a thing of the past.
This would be terrible for our planet, so we must work hard to reduce global warming.

THE WATER CYCLE
My watery friends and I are involved in a nonstop trip around the Earth called the water cycle!

Let's start here! Heat from the sun makes water evaporate into gas called **water vapor**.
Water vapor rises into the air. Higher up, the air is cooler, and it can't hold all the water vapor. So the vapor condenses from a gas into tiny liquid water droplets that form clouds.
Wooo! Rain and snow fall back down to the ground when the clouds can't hold any more water.
The water drains into rivers and lakes through their watershed.

Some water soaks into the ground and becomes groundwater.
Rivers flow back to the ocean, and the cycle begins again!
All of the water on Earth is involved in the water cycle.
None of it can ever be lost and no extra water can ever be added. It's just us forever and ever!
35

UNAVAILABLE FRESH WATER

Remember when I told you that fresh water only makes up about three percent of water on Earth? Well, I've got some bad news for you...

...nearly all of that fresh water is unavailable to us! Let's take a look at where it's hiding away.

It's trapped in frozen glaciers and ice caps ...

... and hidden deep below the surface in groundwater ...

... and in permafrost – a permanently frozen layer found underground in cold parts of the Earth.

Some fresh water is also up in the atmosphere as part of the water cycle.

36

Only about one-third of one percent of fresh water is easily available to use. This is the water found in lakes, rivers, and wetlands.

And we can't even use all of that water, because some of it is polluted! Yuck!

Shortages and pollution of fresh water are serious problems around the world. So don't take me for granted!

Fresh water is a precious resource that we need to protect and use sensibly!

WEIRD AND WONDERFUL WATER

The Dead Sea, located in the Middle East, is the lowest lake on Earth, sitting at over 1,400 feet (427 meters) below sea level.
It's called the Dead Sea because it's too salty for anything to live in it, apart from bacteria!
The salt makes it excellent for floating!
If you love lakes, head to Canada!
Not only is it the country with the most lakes, it is home to more lakes than all the other countries combined!

The Lambert Glacier in Antarctica is the longest on Earth, measuring over 250 miles (402 kilometers). Despite its size, it's one of the fastest glaciers, with some parts moving over 2,600 feet (792 meters) a year!

What an incredible world of water! So wat-er you waiting for? Go out and see it for yourself! Bye for now!

WORDS TO KNOW

aquifer a layer or bed of soil and rock that can yield useful amounts of ground water.

basin an area of land that is lower than its surroundings.

delta the mass of earth and sand that collects at the mouth of some rivers. A delta usually has three sides.

ecosystem all of the living things in an area and the way they affect each other.

estuary the wide part of a river as it meets the sea.

glacier a large river or sheet of ice that moves slowly.

global warming a gradual increase in the overall temperature of Earth's atmosphere.

groundwater water that collects under Earth's surface.

ice sheet a glacier that covers a large area of land.

iceberg a large block of ice that floats in the ocean.

lake a large area of water surrounded by land.

meander a curve in a river.

ocean a very large area of salt water.

permafrost land that is permanently frozen beneath the surface.

pollution damage to the land, water, or air caused by harmful waste.

pond a small area of fresh water.

river fresh water that flows across the land and into the ocean, a lake or another river.

salt water water that contains salt, as found in oceans and seas.

stream a channel of flowing water smaller than a river.

tributary a smaller river that flows into another river or lake.

water vapor water in gas form.

waterfall when water falls from a higher point to a lower point.

watershed the area of land drained by a river or lake.

wetland an area of land that is particularly wet.

www.ingramcontent.com/pod-product-compliance
Lightning Source LLC
Chambersburg PA
CBHW041052050726
47599CB00018B/2118